Edition Schott

Antonio Vivaldi

ca. 1678 – 1741

Concerto

for Violin and String Orchestra
für Violine und Streichorchester

opus 3/6, RV 356
A minor / a-Moll / La mineur

Edited by / Herausgegeben von
Gustav Lenzewski

ED 3695
ISMN 979-0-001-04417-2

Parts available
Orchesterstimmen erhältlich

www.schott-music.com

Mainz · London · Berlin · Madrid · New York · Paris · Prague · Tokyo · Toronto
© 1939 SCHOTT MUSIC GmbH & Co. KG, Mainz · Printed in Germany

VORWORT

In vorliegender Neuausgabe des a-Moll Violinkonzertes von Vivaldi sind die spärlichen in den Abschriften enthaltenen Spielanweisungen im Violinpart ergänzt worden im Sinne der zeitgemäßen Spieltechnik des frühen 18. Jahrhunderts. Da sich die eigentlichen Solopartien in den schnellen Sätzen (ähnlich wie in einem Concerto grosso) aus dem *Tutti* herauslösen, stehen in dieser Ausgabe auch die Tutti-Violinen nur in der Violinstimme. Das Klavier übernimmt möglichst getreu nur die übrigen weniger bewegten Orchesterstimmen, ergänzt durch die aus der Bezifferung sich ergebenden harmonischen Füllungen. Im langsamen Satz werden mit Rücksicht auf den schnell verklingenden Klavierton bei Haltenoten und Überbindungen der Oberstimme einige Töne wiederholt angeschlagen.

Gustav Lenzewski

PRÉFACE

Dans cette nouvelle édition du concerto de Vivaldi les quelques indications que l'on rencontre dans les copies manuscrites de la partie de violon ont été complétées dans le style de l'époque, en tenant compte de la technique dont on disposait au début du 18e siècle. Les parties solo des mouvements rapides se détachant des *tutti*, comme c'est le cas dans les concerti grossi, on a seulement mentionné les tutti dans la partie de violon. On a transcrit au piano, le plus exactement possible, les parties de l'orchestre se mouvant plus lentement en complétant encore les harmonies données par la basse chiffrée. A cause des liaisons de la mélodie et de la durée relativement courte du son du piano, on s'est vu obligé de partager certaines notes du mouvement lent, en les faisant rejouer à nouveau.

Gustav Lenzewski

PREFACE

In this new edition of Vivaldi's A minor violin concerto the meagre indications in the violin part in the copies have been augmented in keeping with the violin technique of the early 18th century. Since the actual solo passages in the fast movements resolve from the *Tutti*, (as in a Concerto grosso) this edition only shows the tutti violins in the violin part. In so far as possible, the piano accompaniment is a true reproduction of the slower orchestral parts harmonized according to the figured indications. In view of the unsustained quality of the piano tone, some of the notes are restruck in the slow movement in order to bind the upper voice.

Gustav Lenzewski

Concerto

a - Moll / La mineur / a minor

Herausgegeben und bezeichnet
von Gustav Lenzewski

Antonio Vivaldi
opus 3 No. 6, RV 356

Allegro

Tutti

Solo

Violine

Concerto
a – Moll / La mineur / a minor

Herausgegeben und bezeichnet
von Gustav Lenzewski

Antonio Vivaldi
opus 3 No. 6, RV 356

Printed in Germany

ED 3695

Schott Music, Mainz 35 863

3

Largo (non troppo) **cantabile**